"For readers who are desperate to remember that writing is a language art and that the painterly musical possibilities of something so quotidian as words can be entirely remade—here is a uniquely gorgeous and sensory voyage. Give up previous ideas of sense for the story that lurks in the fleshy cracks and crevices of linguistic exhilaration. Read on!"

—Thalia Field

"*An Inch Thick* is yr body n its emissions n its sensations n the things outside that come into contact, almost swooping in from blind spots catching u by surprise,—the leaf brushing yr ear fuzzily as it drops to ground, the aphid tickling the edge of yr eyelash, flanks pressed by gentle jaw a warm soft scaly rough,—sometimes sth else:: sth like being tumbled by waves a bit roughly but not unpleasantly,—more like yr at the mercy of a power far greater being exercised cat-like:: toying w yr submitted lil °sof body an excited °fly rubbing forearms habitually gleefully seated upon °overripened fruit {broadcasting body scent (of lover last or mos memorable)}"

—Tilghman Alexander Goldsborough

"Looking up after finishing *An Inch Thick*, I see the people around me suddenly defamiliarized, like the beings in this sci-fi Bildungsroman. They're wet, thing-like, inherently sexual, potentially hazardous, infinite in their stinking: they're human, that is—perfectly human, at last. I can still smell Theo Ellin Ballew's sentences, buoyant and sopping, bubbling up like gasses from a primordial soup. They smell like Beckett at his strangest, like stabs at love, like unwashed bodies coming into contact, orienting each other toward quantum futures of gut-wrought potential. *An Inch Thick* splatters the world as we know it with bodily fluids in order to make it reflect back in new colors. This is a sublimely fleshy book, and it nobly defies categorization."

—Kit Schluter

. . .

"*An Inch Thick* is a sweet-tempered spade. Spade because it's solid and piercing, and sweet-tempered because it sieves like a swollen digit, hotly overwhelmed with its own fluidity, testing both saltwater and soil for their temperature. It is cognizant, unashamed, and deserving of its coolness and the cool things it scratches, and its hotness and the hot things it scratches, deserting home for quick and slight immersions in candy, in lips, in remark. *An Inch Thick* is undeniably a great kisser."

—Chanté L. Reid

"Always at sea, and fiercely present in their visceral homewaters, this poet of cybernetic revolution takes us into the belly of the beast, generously giving us to share. A tumultuous experience."

—John Cayley

"*An Inch Thick* attends with love to the sensations that we would prefer to ignore. Tenderly, precisely, it ventures into thirst and flab, drool and stench. Theo Ellin Ballew has created a new lexicon for the senses. In doing so, they articulate a new ethics of care, of celebration even, for what we otherwise might be tempted to call the abject body. Like Jonah inside the whale, T.E.B. guides us through the insides of our experience."

—Eli Payne Mandel

AN INCH THICK

AN INCH THICK

THEO ELLIN BALLEW

ORNITHOPTER PRESS   CHEVY CHASE

First Edition

Published by Ornithopter Press
www.ornithopterpress.com

ISBN 978-1-942723-18-9

Library of Congress Control Number: 2024937468

Design by Mark Harris

[Character . . .]

to my mom

AN INCH THICK

[Character Is Born Into Brand-New Upcycled Modular World.]

All of us were there in the throat of that fish it was squeezing, thrusting, and hot. Thrashing, there we were, hot.

Our hipbones were pegged one bone to the next, and the tightness would not let them slip. They were pinching like the pressing of things that can't be compressed and they were reaching through the skin. They were reaching through the cartilage. They were touching each others' porous hardnesses, like fingers stone pointing and solid.

The saliva, it was flooding; it was making us stick and smell like ass; it was coating our cartilage from our hipbones pushed back and it rose up to our lower lips; it rose up to our tongue-tips, salty, slimy, to the bottom edges of our noses (up-inclining) as we saw that mouth above us parting, in one last gasp of air and as the gills below us withered, we knew so well, like so sandy selfish and alone.

If you open the blinds, you'll burn the stench out. Remember rot emits no smoke that sticks. And that to sight, shape is all that separates a shiny thing from a wet one. And you're the shallow static of skin holding a swell. And you're holding light like ice, but dry.

Seeds or drops of bone: you are square and they roll across you, high-pitched along your inner sides. You rattle, firm around the fruit flies. You ripen, preparing to move.

I woke with breath lip-thick.

My thick breath woke ready.

To be cut by candy into lightly coughing over the ashes of cigarettes in liquid green and floating.

Walls swelling like purpling (I wish this to a purpling volume.)

Swelling like purpling, and dry.

Damp like my head bit straight through the hair and we heard it, translucent against teeth.

Walls swelling like, in this heat.

And all just waiting to, come, to a humming.

[Character Has Lived Many Lives (a Slut).]

Inside I'm chicken bones and outside I'm candy, they say that though I swear my lips are full—though my fingertips, I swear they're full. ("[My] chicken bones inside reach to be felt—[I] feel them, believe they're fingers.")

Frosting doesn't stick when it leaves the tube so quick: crumbed edges lean right through it. On a foundation of such crisp thickness, my lips… say something dense.

"Inside the sting stuck deepest down in [my] ear—one day we found a wishbone there—lifted it. Like butter, [my] collarbones split."

A cantaloupe like a buzz cut or a wolf, sketched, up to the full-palmed feeling touch: all heads:

All guilts before others spill into one bin and each spill lifts up former spills' scents. The only logic of jealousy that has any dignity is: let my skin be a solid nonporous case. So you spent your lives watching your cells for shedding. And though you're here spilled together into solid fruit-fuzzy, though you marble in this hand ever-shifting to throw: though your spins in distant airways will only wind you more tightly: still your surveillance has a right.

Eyeballs on me like oranges in a bag and I'm a hand reaching in. The bag, it's plastic and green. The oranges they are green. The bag is a net, a stringy green net and just like me it is bursting. Eyeballs in sockets rolling deep like my sex; it's hard this life like oranges on skin. Hard this life and deep, man those eyeballs go so deep, and fruits are the true new the pure new the full new and more than any complicated plate they induce at the tip of the very first taste: the still desire to vomit.

Of all the things I could possibly want to do, there are none, here, right now. My only hope is to put my face on pause to pose a moment of sexy distraction—behind my bunch of melons, one sliced. "Turn your phone on vibrate; let me touch you." Either way, eventually, I'll be along, on the rounds of some steamed thick stream.

"The stench of their feet was nearing that of their cunt and they squatted, to smell them, some days. They only liked floors where their feet felt heat, and their laundry all went in together. They were one of those compelled to the vicious uprooting of self, floating skinny, on hot ponds. Somewhere someone said, 'remember your feet's strength,' because strength is followed by heat. But their feet kept fading (always too sharp) and the floors! only had so much to give."

I kept an olive on my floor, I liked to see it roll. It wouldn't ever go bad.

Every book she lent me was candy-colored and too solid for my feet; but she cooked only rough things strange to my teeth with heat, and bounce, and fading. When the bones came out my mouth I'd stained them pink. She kept it warm in there she said, "all for [me]," and that's why I didn't want her at my back.

Whoever fucks me remembers that I am from the desert, but only that first time. I'd been trying to grab my own left thigh; I thought maybe, finally, I'm making a sculpture; I thought finally, I'm working with the solid. I thought of ways to bring candy, solid, to my face, like blue glass or salmon veils. I thought of salmon, baked, and left in others' apartments, where I'd slept warm and never woke in sweat.

[Character Loves, Loses – 1.]

In some great big sea rolling all the waves rolling humorless and soft, soundless soft, will I wait, you, will I wait on you, will I await, as I hum into my ears. As my ears hum like seashells, into my ears, such cushions, so dearly used. In some great big sea battle of elbows and teeth, on a neck, in a street. I'll wait with bones emerging, such seashells from sand, so hard, and so undiscerning. Will I see you, here, here? And what salve would you put on my cheeks. What sands would it on me sink. In what pores would it so suddenly seep in what scratches would it seethe, boiling, burning, what dissolving would reveal what teeth. What exists that's not great big and here. I need to touch big immediately, here. I need to touch you in any elbow, eye jutting out, unwitting bones sprouting, here. In any thirsts here surprising, flesh needing to be undone, what will be undone, kid, and with what's this haste, what flavors of your bones have I yet still to taste and what curves will those tastes here take. I'm here thirsting, with my belly, I'm here humming throat to throat, I'm here full wild in words you cannot comprehend. I'm right here, rolling waiting, waves still swallowing themselves, so great, big and so ever in.

And isn't everything grown just some miracle of the infinite forgotten to fester in stream-less ponds. And doesn't everything grown leave behind so much, like skin, soft and spread, in depths.

And your love it will be your new depression. It will hold you, make you immobile. It will make your head immobile. It will make your head not remember a single thing, stuck repeating this one sensation. Repeating this one sensation, in one single space, repeating and not allowing an outside.

Because love will be, like depression, your only sensation, love will be like the good planet Earth. It will hold you tight like gravity like the only planet Earth and it will be the one use for photos.

Like depression your love will make: you stay in bed, like depression there you'll question: your muscles' weight, like in depression you'll forget: all feeling built by process because your love, like depression, it will have no process; like depression your love will be: ever always right there and to your love like to depression you'll be ever always there, ever just outside, and always in, ever open and unstopping all your fixed repetition all that boredom in and out and all of that truth: blood, like your one single move.

It smelled like cigarettes, outside the earthquake. From our stillness on the sidewalk, we two looked up, and we saw it all swinging, here and there. We saw its skeletal plant leaves, shuddering. We saw its windows just like water lapping. We saw it from the sidewalk where we stood on that face, its mountainous features gathered toward one single space and as ever, obscuring the view.

That earthquake's shaking surfaces reflected our gazes like the inside of a cookie wrapper creased. We were two silver sprawling toward every single crumb, fun, homeward bound.

And every pore of yours was some high leaf's sudden sprouting—all highest leaves' sprouting sudden in one single point—beneath the very cold sun. A pore a sprouting hook, a velcro strand that shuddered, a great big honey lake where my steps sunk all my legs—and above us was that sun, ever freezing. And below us was that lake, real ever sticking and sneezing and above us, that world, suddenly full of drawn-on faces, quiet, there, and quaking.

Suddenly slipping like sliced it'll be gone, this screen, against which I hang. This screen pressed across every curve and flat of me, this screen, cooling every inch. Like a slice, sudden, it will part. It will be gone and the corners of my mouth will spread, both the two corners of my mouth will open they will fall, deep into my cheeks.

And we only know extremes through the approach. Of a color, we never see its peak. I am, something and done, I am, oh something and done, I am something, in it and done and it's uttered... not a single word.

Sliced, gone, like the skin of my own stomach, like losing every layer of the skin of my own stomach, sliced, out, like quick shortcut vomit, or the sudden up-tugging of a rug.

Do you ebb and flow like swallowing do you pop and spread like a tin can's top do you meet yourself in full circle release. Years ago you asked how I had perfect teeth and I spent years thinking about what you'd seen. My eye sockets they are peeling. My feet are bleeding from shower shoe cuts. But here are all the sweet ways of sucked seeds on tongues slipping; here are all the ripe carrots that just like mangos are softening; and here's me, having loved you, all like a dog's tongue: out, gross, and drooling.

The sound of shit's end like metal scraping metal or being cut, easy as butter. And the doors shutting somewhere, inside or elsewhere, and each shower stream shuttling like solid. Can the water gallop straight out this glass bottle? Out, over boring air? And your hand across my ass, like plastic or like porn, funny, and not hot, as ever. And then I vociferate deep down in your ear, coaxing like a rock or a stone. My shoulder-span stretches across the round of your vision and my collarbones hold you, just right. You congeal as small and simple as a piece of red lint like soft, but not deep. You're red and sweet as the fullest removed death and you taste of false lemoned pine. Your burning blooms only with the hairs on your high hairline that are mine, and single file.

Knife slithering dropped, onto a floor, it scattered, away, to the other side of the earth, and stuck there, still, a tree. Its leaves grew in every direction. Its roots grew straight down, straight sharp down, they were coming through all those layers of tight heat. They were coming, through the earth, back to us.

Where you're smashed-in and flabby as a hand's old palm, more smashed-in and flabby even than an old hand's palm: you've left yourself there breathing on our wall. Your face is collapsed and bent-back as the skin between two fingers; I wouldn't go past your chin's peak. I lay one hand lightly on your exhaled thigh, as you breathe, in, and out.

And I wait for those roots to emerge in all their bits. I wait for them to slit, through our thick floor tiles, their metal, as always, the tightest. Their points are so narrow they're invisible for yards yes I'll feel them before I see them, today. Yes today, here they come. Yes today this same day that you tack yourself up as a knife from my hand, like a snake drops, yes you feel them, settling, today right in, as I reach, here, begging ever, and so sharpened that I flex.

You arrived in that world and there was every single love you had lived, balled into one. Yes there I was but I could not speak. I'd lost my cold by contracting a flu but my hand still leaked out ice. A light bulb was hanging from my ceiling as ever, and I'd shrunk down enough to be it.

And it was over, all around. Even the air was over. It was over, everything, over, spent: in that air of exhales and swallowed coughs, where I could swing, but never move. I mouthed: so, did these wars feed you? I have been here, hanging, a grape about to burst and you come, less than a fog.

Insides slaughtered like smashed by pressures stinging in their emptiness in the shapes of a face. I'd had the most untouched thing, with position. And now wide went the fallouts in every deep silent cut; slow, and making space. The walls they straddled my walking. And the water-making was such a spread-armed throwing thing that my head swelled to smear those solids. I was thinking before sleeping that I might dream a baby holding an egg, that I had hard-boiled.

It is likely that time never feels like its measurements even when insides do have widths steady. I wanted a towel dark-red and inch-thick like what I seep, to hold me to my size. But it drifted in bits into inner elbows I was left with just lint yes and the watching of my toes as they turned from short fingers into shapes. I said of them, "This at least is age."

There was a loosening one day when I thought I missed instead a baby within the naive exit of sleep. But soon I saw it was only, just the same, scraped down to a throat's start of milky breath.

That absence was the thing most scraped down to the bone of all sharp things in the world. It was gape-flashing everywhere forever. It made the chests like being juiced, stinging in their citrus, while lying on their backs they bubbled up.

It gave everything such a width.

And thoughts of that fucking brought on such cowers because where was there presence so sharp. Sharp like the widest most zoomed-in static like the highest throat sounds lasting long as exhalations and just floating, shallow now, in all ways too narrow, somewhere behind the solid.

Like oil what stains is unlikely to rot and that, there is what we want.

There are people whose presence is inevitable as ants but who shock like a centipede every time.

You gave that body a reason to be solid, for centuries; now wrapping paper held it in place.

Let's pause to understand the fact that stop lights last one minute, and sometimes more, sometimes less.

I was killed in a coincidence after many attempted murders, and that's how the treasure was found. It was a jar, stuffed between my elbow and my waist.

Could I have had something so big, for so long, and lost it?

I'd tried to switch my inborn fantasies out for safer ones, at least once every year of that life. But these attempts always turned out to be pretend and I was always the last to know, finding: that I could only survive off chips (of any kind) stolen—and hung up in my coat. Then one day, once, my attempt was real—I got that jar—I held it—and now it's gone.

[Character Fucks Around in the Open Air, En Route to Reality.]

Hey onion skins the driest skins and the sharpest, hey give up to me your pile. I will press it, between my knees. Sometimes I'll blow away some flaked-off wing; sometimes, I'll wing it, into a bird. And the birds I will tuck them back behind my ear where they will rest and whistle out a water....

They whistle out a water that's warm as a shower and that sticks to one stream down my arm. Don't forget the fizz that grows there, or: the goods you left in its airs: thicker... cardboards strewn, with markings at all angles and gashes where they've been burst through.

And meanwhile nothing shakes as vibrantly as the extremes, like skin-and-bones or cellulose fat—I have always prided myself on my contrast—no, no one shakes like me.

Bird I swear on my grave and on my mother's first tooth, ever and ever, amen: thou shalt not waste away in paper towels like this, a present, ready for school. Thou shalt mind these swears, these promises given, these airborne things plunked here like pillows.

I will tell the truth, the whole and nothing but, amen God and pluck me up. Like the feather of a bird all sounding its cluck and puffing up its chest in the wind. Ruffling up its chest, its furry soft chest like a hand on itself in caress.

I will hold you in my lap, my bird, my child, I will hold you here just like that. I will watch your paper towels for leaks in their patterns, like pixels my present you ready for school?

Are you ready to attest, you bird, to our goodness, are you ready to attest to our faith? In my salt-swollen fingers I settle your sweet bones, skin and bones, flesh like age, or elbows.

I'll tell the truth with it all stuffed in my mouth. I'll tell the truth with your bones spurting out my mouth, with your skin, dripping like drool. Thou shalt learn the depths that are mine. And in that abyss thou shalt sprout in sin, a gun, set off just like that.

Your taste of tang latches onto the obvious fight, while rocks snatch mesh outside. As in your kitchen walls clean up what you produce, to keep your body together.

Not that deep in the fridge, but close like gum chewed: (even sleeping you could feel the steady touching of that hand: it can only hang:) a bag of artichokes, pumping without chests. And if we scrape it, away?

Happened a grand total of once and to the herbs not at all: a sparrow squished pollution off the leaves. If you sow it the cats don't know it but if you set it the cats will get it, is it too much water or too much heat? Are roots winding, smelling sweet? Simply wrap your four fingers around the bottom, like it's dough or a soft-bodied insect. Light green and pink waxy wool foam: kills naturally while I'm wanting to fuck someone. I spray vinegar, Google "does vinegar kill mint," and find an affirmative answer.

Feeling a grape, round in my eye, it's been fermenting there for minutes. It's hard as a peach, my fingers hold it, they try to pry.... The cotton candy swaths of sky take their time, but I've seen others eat—I call to them: could they come suck this eye?

Because water-blue like not-blue like clear, is my belly; a bit of a wave, a turning in no direction.

As I try to accustom to this crawl of ants or flies, on all sides, or it's only a strand of hair.

Soon I will hold a car-warming party, for my baby. You'll all be there, elbows sticking out.

Put some butter on your serious, I now say, to those who believe in the efficacy of cleaning. Unlike them, I am wise. But still every time I've shivered, I couldn't not. "Sponges," I repeat, "they're just to knock things off."

Don't worry about my feet; they know how not to swallow.

And I only ingest the strictest hedonism; nothing so sterile as that.

[Character Misses Their Mother, Inside Walls.]

"Pain [is]" always "a revelation." Drooling in your insides. Requiring space where there couldn't have been and slimy. Producing slime out of nothing, stubbornly excreting, just spilling dripping inside with no regard. Squeezing intervening in no air to make it flakes, in mornings, flicked away.

From your liver inside your lower back it's drooling. It is seeping, down into your groin. It is titillating your nerves, it's opening them up, you are wet, with this drool, or you've come. From your high thigh muscles it's drooling. Be they flexed, or relaxed. It goes down, to your feet, it fills them like shoes in wide muddy puddles, sunk.

You have wanted to lay down. Your head is very light. Your finger-tips are too swollen to scratch a single thing they sprawl layered, beneath your face palms-down.

Do you eat bananas, they asked you one day. And you said, "but when I do, it's just the flesh." And with your sharp skinny plastic spoon you sliced yours open, and it crackled and popped sinewy, down.

Edges lip-outing like frills but slow-motion like in liquid; thick, soft. I am a sheet; thin, all edges. I am thread-bare from bones here I'm bits I bear my own weight, there will always be air that hurts these teeth. There will be bites, into this cold.

How can my pole slant into that line, how can I rhythm into that speed. I was once stampeded by my own hurry: and some words can sometimes be absurdly short as consonants: and now now, cover me to the quick.

There were the cracklings and the crawlings from the floor side of the ceiling and the trippings on the innards of an unspun bobbin wandering. There were the misplacings of a wallet, on the minute. There were the fevers mounting spiraled and the pains all spiking up, and suddenly sliding, on muscles out of joint. There were the ingredients irreverent of meals. There were the several water bottles, half-filled. There were the doorbells, buzzing, arriving riding on the wind weighted by car sides and tires, brushed by. There were the scratches on sunglasses sprawled like river rocks and smudged from all of the hands, from all of the times, shades spent done and filled with the perishable and: reflecting all the same.

I didn't know words existed that could so fully shut me up.

Once I weeded up a bunch of floor moss and tossed it and to this day I feel the loss. But still I apply lipstick to teach my mouth to sit amongst my cookie boxes, cereal, and mirrors. Here, there's me, past my best-rehearsed fantasy as two freckles emerge for the first time from my ass cheeks, ten from my thighs. I feed, off all my sleeplessness...

So my fog machine and I can puff out.

Spread butter over the lesions of this city; they're on the inner walls but you see them, through the windows. You think that they might be freshly cut flowers, because of the way they hover. Pour butter, bury them, into the walls, and tile them over neatly, or not. What comes through that mortar will only be color and will make no figurative designs. Don't worry, only color, pushing out beating, with eyes only to plump.

“I left my house.

“I don’t know what I did to deserve this.

“I’m going outside.” (Do you want a drink? I said.)

“I’d rather have a nervous breakdown.” (Do you want a drink? I said.)

My tomato rolled off my plate onto the blankets; I was only trying to eat it.

A notebook ever upside down and it’s red the pen is red its ink is red. The bed on which it lies is red. The sun in this window it is red or it’s a moon, red and too swollen to scratch.

What do you do when the person on the line starts choking and the call gets cut off.

I left my house, you’d said. I don’t know what I ever did. You’d been entering a leafy road in some country far away you’d been describing the leaves so much like boats and dust patterned by rain and did that dust firm up in your throat?

On my bed my toes tangled with my extension cords and I thought of ways they might be undone. My teeth were huge in my mouth. My mouth was so many walls. My lips were red, inside and red outside and pale puce, along the edges.

And you your greatest power was always your fear, infinite, out there, and complete.

I ate the contents of my room and now I'm stronger with less to carry. I'd been overwhelmed by how much my hands were everywhere, like my ass-sides and the short edges of the shelves. And meanwhile constantly getting blinded by those bright things behind my eyelids. I never could figure out their origins. But I imagined they were the fallouts from your constant transpositions, in my head, from huge to wire thin.

Anyway, now that's all fixed.

Today yes I even slipped on my clothes, with all their strange tugging and scratching; clothes that bit me picked me here, there. As I reached, out, for the spice... in the grand race to the corner store as the sun shone through the window, on my red simmering head. The tea would be: just right.

Later those clothes were hanging, shedding their wet weight of tea wiped up from my thrice-spilled cup; they were posed, still, on the doorknobs. They were waiting, ready to slip.... Dust was sugar dissolving and it seeped sweet into wooden floors. And me, nearby watching, my hair there crunching, each strand shifting on wood loud like sand.

This room I've left it open with candles ugly and unchosen, I've let them burn, as they were lit. There's no mirror no full mute harshness (that desires dirt but blocks), no mirror and no perfection, no end and no destroying, no mirror where the only way things go is out:

[Character Loves, Loses – 2.]

Bright golly great it is there in a round it is silky and in colors it is bright yes like vintage it is, without shame. Bright golly great it is nodding so timely it is nodding with timing that presses just right it is nodding like the most correct notes placed correctly at just, the just right depths. It is nodding and I swear that it could tip. I try to hold it in my hands like a thumb covers a sun: if it tips, I can only watch.

Really a strong jug a plastic a round now rippled round me rippling oh a strange, oh, a steady. Is it corny that I'm eyes like fish to you man, like in other people's sockets shining caught.

It is fishy god it's serious yeah dumb dumb serious yeah caught, like moving I'm not moved. I'm only turned caught in rippling steady shifting like an eye, in some socket, all moved smooth and shine.

And in this steady how so oh about to fall. And in this steady how I flex, reverent, against all possible drip.

Centered in baseballs in stumbling in ankles, tilting, full of weight. Ankles are cotton like squeaking and stuffy; toes, of uncertain number. Ankles or the world's most overwhelmed corners, self-conscious and so shown: or rickety balloons filled with breath forever sinking except for the times when they're kicked.

Beneath my baby, built up of breakfast apps.

Apps, meaning appetizers.

But a herd of ants descends on my collarbones. They dig in a sheet, toward my ass. We call out through our one thousand red throats—for soda, or something cold.

And I grab sand out from my belly sides; and it drips from my hands, in sour peach.

Whenever and wherever my nose reaches a certain angle I smell canned soup freshly opened. Like how I keep remembering, with great velocity, losses I'd forgotten. I will invent an ending with duration.

Until then I'll spoon out the right doses of entertainment... and avoid the mouthfuls of shit steam.

They should write a book that traces the lines of influence that led to each of your mannerisms. I'd sit with it.

What I'm in is tame, complete, as a sky and won't leave. It tucks in storms, they're stacked flat. I fester any distraction into some member of you... and how can I buy a sky treats, from here? The packaging you left is in the hem of my foot and it grows with each step. Such massive goodness, you're fuzzy at the edges, as again and again you plagiarize my drunk talk from the view on the roof of my mouth.

Your inner sweet is so big it hits the left side of your hip and flees out the bottom of your right thigh. Your feet are stiff and brittle as the dusty tops of metal and they pry, through papered windows.

What kind of baby crashes into you and dies I said "he crashed into me."

You can always spot youth by the way it looks around like it's only just arrived; nothing so unsexy as a tourist.

But there's a layer of your face always trying to hide itself, and so still you look older than you are.

Within a cell spit sprouted but down like rooting like roots with fists at their ends. Fists that sent electric to quick it all up—electric made of spit dirty and hard as the clumped… hair of a cat. The roots had bulbous side-leaves made of tragedies fit for centuries and hanging, on like red heat. They held on like infection hit right in the chest, binding hot like what hangs from the center of a chest and the cell made room, silently and sweet.

(There was a bubble a huge bubble and three horses racing after it and on the horses' sides were painted stars and on the peaks of the stars were bubbles—)

—And regardless, you're there at any distance.

Sometimes I stop talking to apologize for adding my wine-colored spit into the mix. We've been building this liquid, for years. One day it'll all boil down to a bone.

Bone in the shape of the torn-off corner of a chip bag.

I'll pay attention to the lining.

Till then I toss and suck on moist cashews and pour out sip-sized portions from bottles opened months ago. When you get to a place with another person where the hurt is in everything: is there no going back? There could be a side of a stadium where we all finish everything we start and I wish so hard that I'm a fact.

You are every wooden floorboard damp rotting and flat, ever flat, flat from the start, no meaning. Rotting, you reveal your light weight. You reveal that you were only ever fiber stacked together and that in certain environs you spread. Will you float, now, in the water that broke you, or are you so consumed now that you'll sink.

I've found your splinters stuck deep in my teeth. They have no taste.

I'll let you go, go, I'll let you go, go, I'll let it go, you were only ever a sky.

You can't eat peanut butter out of the jar while drinking water out of a peanut butter jar—he'd said it slowly, so I could hear. I don't remember the rest.

But what happened there happened again in a dream and then I felt the pain.

Now I dip in salt, and not salt water with my bread, my own wet there to stick. I will feel through this, "back to myself."

I will nerve-floss my heart-strings until they are stretched, so they don't clock every tug they can. I will do this every morning, and every night, and then finally I'll throw out the last used condom on my floor and like a spoon, then I'll be clean.

I don't care if the sun spreads out sweet from her bubble: she's an empty piece of gum so she folds in candy corn, once a day—it calms her down.

It's what she does, and I'd do the same.

Because all I've ever wanted was to be good at maintenance. And once again, I've not managed. Now you have your facts for comfort; what do I have; I have my theorizing of the workings of a humidifier (—to shoo out the chance of you in my bed) and—

The knowledge that we don't remember the extremes.

•

That vocabulary is my phantom limb….

Vocab that tried so hard for so long to say truth; but truth lasts forever and its length is such a shame and in fatigue from the telling, I lied.

Also, in the interest of time.

A really long, skinny, hot hot pink limb: and scalding, when I move to see it. Limb, where's your father? Who wants sons! My own body, when it's sexy, reminds me of you and yet I'm trapped in the shape of my face, at tables, thirsty for and scooping up salt. I'll bloat till I have enough space.

Phantom limb of words and my own moaning… if only the un-sounding start.

Tender as a serrated knife on a wrinkled lemon, I'm tender; the first lemon water in years.

It was the biggest kiss I had ever had, ha. I could have walked around in it. I wanted the smell to be: from a mold and not leave and there was hope in how it changed with the season.

But that was just a cherry on its own on the top.

Now every cubed inch of me could swallow eight gallons, of water, salty water, or could be anything.

"I loved it when you slept, meant you were in my arms." Hey taste, could you be sleep? Come to me.

[Character Time-Travels Back to Someone's Sturdy Home,
Engages an Angel.]

A lemon tree—a god—someone said left from agriculture—my nails into her rinds will architect the round... through the window, I get there quicker. (I will become a very good driver.)

Fill, slow, my gums. I'll fall till it opens out beneath. I'll fall hanging held, by my four wet fingers in a row, sick there till: the well opens out beneath.

I knew the home-not-home could only be some kind of red but I didn't know how quick its sky would shift. I turn my brow I shift my tongue to let air in beneath and sunrise flips up gleam. And every object I bump into is one I once shed and it was mine or the mirrors stand too tall.

And I see my place and it's still built for me two-times or rather the shard between two people only solid when two-times; one, I am slick without bounds I am: only... for my place to slip.

A wild car face like a car running wild, but maraschino sweet nonetheless. Maraschino car as in I've loved a shirley temple and car rides used to put me to sleep. A wild car face I'm out the way. A cheap speed face but the sweetest sweet; water it or it spreads like pink cotton. Water it so it won't be cotton candy, and tuck it in underneath the sheets.

My hands tuck in but my torso seeps out. It takes the top left door.

It goes through maraschino sweet sweetness thick like fast tires like their smell if I brake quick and force them down into shedding, pressed shedding rubber pressed into a gone so smooth like a father, or what escapes me.

Upon return to a fantasy everything holds its shape.

And dust is as before in sky-gradient.

And colors fill out the same spaces on the tongue… only textures have changed place.

There are people the exact shape of gesture that you love, but posed at the wrong angle. They are perfect, only in fucking. And there are warmths that increase when you sit in them still, and there are others that do not.

A sanity could be made of these ill-fitted tracings, these repetitions with consonants misplaced; these returns, skewed, so you're not facing what you visit or there's some side in impossible size.

We cut it off to try to understand. After the rain its tufts were openings and they let out, thick, onto my dried used tea bags stuck to it.

A year before a face was aged in just one spot, beside the nose, in the side-socket. The eye was in no way closed it was like the hands were, like flinging: she was just trying to speak.

And damp trash sitting, not so long, smelling maybe like salt water. And someone saying, falseness puffs her every inch.

She said at first she couldn't tell if I was hopeless or just cocky. In her nightmares it seemed she was a very deep sleeper so when she woke she said, what could have happened. She spread lotion on her skin like putting on a fitted sheet, in a mirror, at night before sleep.

"I don't need to look both ways, I hear the cars coming. Or my eye-corners are strong. [...] You've grown another mouth it needs my mouth. [...] Their name was a strange version of a common name and I try to remember it at least once a week."

(Start fucking me and I'll start picking up the habits of your mom, I think. It happens every time.)

"And I don't know who taught me to menstruate soot like this, but they did pause in their lesson, as I sent a text, and we lowered our eyes to hear me read it: 'If we are born the first time we fall in love, I am eight times your age.'"

Every day her watching got deeper into me. She was staring through my old rough bark. Clogging, she caressed herself into me until she was part of my body.

Then I went to grasp her dry green veins, got her sudden, serious look. She was not her best.

I wanted color past that of a just-rolled-over sun and the air woke up, for half an hour. I saw her, swarming with details. She was curled, and hanging in listening. Laughing at her urgency, I said, "there it is!" and our facial expressions sat up. I tried to expunge my tree from my mind—and took her to hide in its shade.

A gasping kind of gorgeous as in I saw it and kept gasping; and then I stripped in my sleep. It's the only thing I do in my sleep. But what I remember is turning down the volume on my headphones, and watching the speech sounds stretch. Gorgeous as in with depth wholly flipped out, from all the rest.

[Character Dies, One Last Time.]

My sea is a pussy it welcomes you warmly. It meows and opens its legs. It purrs like ripples like waves when it's petted, down by a hand; it moves there so subtly like laughing.

When I am alone I think of palms pressing down onto my chest. Above my breasts. I imagine me crying into a lap like milk, and one seems to be opening her legs, I seem to be falling, one, seems to be swinging her hand from my shoulders down to my waist, up to my hips, back down et cetera I'm lapping it up, under it all, like milk again, or like water.

My sea seeps out of my mouth sometimes, like milk, and I am sorry. It says words like "sad" and it says words like "sex," it says words like "object," like "pain." It laughs very hard, at these words, and other words, and if it hadn't hidden its face I would have seen it happening or maybe only if I had looked.

I have wanted to be a ship; I have wanted to be the shore; I have wanted to be some words that are read, every single one. I have wanted to be an object and to feel my own bounds, I have wanted to knock them against tables against faces, I have thought about clotheslines and all the water seeping out, I have pawed at the air in hopes of catching it I have done this by myself, in air that seems infinite, and if you were there if you were anyone you would have only been the ground.

Here is what I am always doing I am always trying to water things down or I am always trying to dry things out, here is what I am doing my bounds keep on being broken. My bounds keep being broken like metaphor like simile like mixing like wrong, wrong, they're wrong. My bounds keep on transforming like what. My bounds keep breaking I break them like welcoming like what they are spreading, open, in their desperation for definition as I am wrung, out, again and again, like clothes, again, or like water.

What a glorious long tide it was, seeping sliding out. A long time, sloping and stirring. Striking at the crests, boiling just slightly, self-strangling with reaching and stretch.

That was what your hand was every second. That was what your pores were, every one single one: long, out, and stretching. Boiling slightly scalding that skin.

That skin or that bark, that trunk hardening down, like a rock or like cement, rolling. Rounding as you climbed it all callous and scratching and breaking thorns off at their roots.

As you gurgled deep down I don't care I don't care through the white wine in your mouth held seething. You were refusing, spitting, to swallow.

You were peeling off the leaves so slow. You were floating them on the sea in your mouth there reeling they were slipping simpering off tripping they were floating cradling the dust and the thorns in the air.

They were landing on your children so bountifully there, so small—and looking up in awe.

The bees, they won't stop their blabbering. They are tired, but cannot land. And the wind swings them onto any cheek freckle hand but they are smug sniffing sights for their honey.

And high as you climb in the end the wind dies, as your stature sinks to an infinitely small size and the bees, then, they preside, on the narrow raised shoulders of your children.

We were twelve years old when the walls tipped in we were twelve years old and then some. We were twelve years old but that couldn't be right and our eyes, they were getting very bad. We were twelve years old or else one hundred and twenty and yes we knew our decimals' place.

We were losing our space and the walls tipped in we were twelve years old, or more. We were twelve, old, or yes one hundred and twenty, and the walls they seemed to tip and touch.

Standing up we saw that they did not. Standing our knees scraping, bones against bones, one hundred twenty years and things were all too close and our skin, it expanded for some space. It folded, searching for space.

And we were sure that everything was in its proper place when we began to feel our skulls through our skins. Yes we felt them through our skins on our foreheads noses chins as between the walls we saw that it was raining. And out we cried goodbye and hi as to our cheeks our stomachs climbed. The nausea would not come unstuck. It was sticking to our skins like plastic wrappers we were twelve years old standing and all we wanted was some space, excuse us, we said, could our nauseas be like tissue paper dissolved in glue or in sweat.

Excuse us, we said, we did not know our place. Our mind was dissolving by the second or the century with our skull showing through like glue. Excuse us, we said, but this floor is too thick, excuse us but hello, twelve and help? Our perspective was dissolving, to a vanishing, point, one hundred two, all roads go there. Our hands were one reaching for our hair. And our skin receded, our skull rinsed in rain, while our mouth, it was quenched, of thirst.

Acknowledgments

The poems on page 34 and page 75 appeared in *Juked*; the poems on pages 13, 22, and 48 appeared in *3AM*; and the poem on page 77 appeared in *Pif Magazine*; all have been altered since original publication.

About the Author

Theo Ellin Ballew is a writer from the U.S. desert. They live in New York, where they also teach cybernetic revolution and direct ORAL.pub. Theo holds an MFA from Brown. Their writing has appeared in various journals and art spaces; more information is on theo.land/.

Milton Keynes UK
Ingram Content Group UK Ltd.
UKHW040300181024
449757UK00001B/189

9 781942 723189